The Longest Chord

The Longest Chord

A Compilation by

Khalid El Bey

New York

To my children; this is for you. Make sure you read it. ☺

CONTENTS

Chapter

Introduction

Life presents each of us with a myriad of challenges. These challenges, some of which are predictable and most of which are not, overwhelm the majority of us each and every day. From the earliest moments in our lives when as toddlers our young minds acquired the ability for comprehension, up and until our golden years leading to our earthly exit, we are all constantly faced with intellectual, emotional, financial, social, political, relationship, family and societal dilemmas with which we have the responsibility to somehow overcome.

This book is a compilation of three books that I had previously published, with some revisions.

These books: The Key to Character, NOW and Love Under Will, were provided with the hopes of helping readers "loosen the shackles". Realizing that each book appears to only cover a portion of one's issues, I thought it would be beneficial for readers if they had access to all three with one purchase.

Each book or part scrutinizes specific areas of life that we all have in common. While each book can stand and has stood on its own, the combining of all three will enable the reader to establish a connection between numerous issues, ultimately identifying a "common theme" or cause; once said cause(s) is identified the reader may be able to zero in and eventually neutralize the source of his or her struggles.

Words on paper are not mechanical (necessarily) and so simply reading the contents of this compilation isn't enough. It still remains our direct responsibility to get a handle on our circumstances. My wish is that you discover a source of strength within these pages and that this moment of discovery marks a turning point in your life for the better.

- Khalid El Bey
  Author

BOOK I

THE KEY TO CHARACTER

THE KEY TO CHARACTER

BY

KHALID EL BEY

DEYEL PUBLISHING COMPANY

217 WEST KENNEDY STREET,
SYRACUSE, NEW YORK [13205]

CREATIVE RESEARCH SOCIETY

SYRACUSE, NEW YORK

ACKNOWLEDGEMENTS

The Author wishes to thank the following individuals who contributed to the manifestation of this book:

Professor Howard Gordon at Oswego State University for sharing his expertise in the proper use of the English dialect.

Carolyn Haughton for providing her thoughts on The Key to Character in its forward.

Dr. Donald C. Sawyer III, who took time while working on his Ph.D. to write the Introduction of this book.

FORWARD

The Key to Character is thought provoking.   It scrutinizes the psyche, social conditioning theory and alleged politically correct norms.   Like being in a courtroom,   the   arguments   presented   by   the prosecuting attorney and the defense attorney to persuade a jury of one's guilt or innocence is largely determined by the most convincing presentation of the evidence and facts. The final outcome does not mean that the truth has prevailed or the majority should rule. That said, the Author challenges the assumption of those who suggest one's self worth has much to do with level of education, the three C's (cash, class and color), worldly possessions (a fine home, luxury cars) and personal relationships (the who's who you rub shoulders with).   Rather, character is about compassion, sensitivity, integrity, respect for self as well as others and the freedom to explore and test what we instinctively feel is different and unique without ridicule.

-    Carolyn Haughton, B.A. Psychology

INTRODUCTION: BECOMING A JEWEL

(Life's perfecting/polishing journey)

I love Hip-Hop! Though the culture has drifted far off the path of its foundation and most of the original tenets are overshadowed by misogyny and violence, the more positive aspects exude intellectual energy and creativity. Some of the great lyricists (Notorious B.I.G., Jay Z, Kanye West) are able to play with words in ways that academically trained scholars can only dream. With that being said I will do as the aforementioned Emcees by 'playing' with the word "character" in this introduction.

Are we living in a world built on character or a world full of characters? Are we a people of great character or are we characters participating in this world's show? I would argue that we live in a society with an abundance of characters that lack character. What do we do about this? With so many worldly influences and external voices telling us how we should act, who we should date, what clothes we should wear, what kind of car we should drive; it takes a strong, self secured individual to put up and hold in place a force-field to block out these negative stimuli. It takes a great deal of effort to go through the day constantly guarding against all that we encounter that is created to influence and control our choices and decisions. If we let down this protective barrier, we run the risk of becoming mindless drones aimlessly wondering the earth until the day we go to the grave. If you are reading this now, you have already taken a step towards beginning or continuing your self-initiating process of improving or perfecting your character, which will then have a positive impact on your circles of influence. The perfection of character is no easy task.   As mentioned earlier, the societal influential machine is a serious force that is not easily defeated. The perfection of character is a painstaking process of continual self examination filled with mental, emotional and spiritual searching and pruning. Many gardeners will tell you a plant that is pruned has the ability to grow faster and stronger than those allowed to grow unchecked or unguided.   The pruning process fosters the removal of distractions, while allowing all positive energies to be transmitted into those areas that are in need of development. The perfecting of character mirrors this pruning process.

As you move along through this process of growing towards self-perfection, be ever mindful of the fact that there will be trials and tribulations. This soul searching may bring a multitude of sensitive areas to the forefront that will need to be dealt with in the appropriate manner. Some of our being has to be fostered and fertilized, while other parts of our self will need to be DESTROYED. A seed dies in the ground before new life can sprout. When you dive into the information that this book provides, be sure to not do so blindly and take every word at face value...that would be religious. Instead, use these words as a catalyst to begin or continue your adventures of self-study, correction, and intellectual attainment. I end this introduction with the words of an African proverb, "A jewel is not polished without rubbing; neither is a person without trials. "Read this book and search for your personal key.

-    Dr. Don C. Sawyer III, Ph. D

Chapter 1

MY MIND OR YOURS

(I live by YOUR standards)

Many times I've had discussions with people, whether it was in an open dialog or forum, or a personal conversation about the differences between what we believe, what we have been conditioned to think or believe and what it is that we actually know. These discussions have led me to think about how people live out their entire lives according to or circled around some idea that someone else had developed. In our lives, these ideas become the principles, the laws or standards by which we measure ourselves and/or by which we live. This type of conditioning exists within all cultures throughout the world; whether related to religion, economics, fashion or any other ideas or images that might attract our attention during any particular phase in our lives. For the most part anybody would say to you that this is fine, to each's own, whatever works for you. My only concern is that with most of what many of us have been conditioned to think, very, very few of us have ever questioned, not just the source of the idea(s), but our reason(s) for accepting the idea(s). Take for instance the touchiest subject of all subjects: religion. I have personally talked to numerous people and have asked them why; why do they think or believe as they do in regards to their respective religions? Quite a few of the initial responses were, "because this is what I want or choose to believe"; but as I questioned further the answers would change to, "because this is what my Mother or Father taught me to believe". Ok, I'll accept that; but where did your Mother and/or Father get the idea(s) from and have they ever questioned their reasons for accepting whatever ideas they have accepted about religion? I doubt it. Nine times out of ten, they are only doing as 'they' were told to do.

Now this is not an attack on religion, for there are numerous ideas, fads, etc., that may be considered customs around which many people base their lives. Let us take a quick look at fashion. The fashion world with all of its glitz and glamour has created a standard, which causes many people around the world to drive themselves insane or into poverty by trying to keep up with the high cost of clothing and jewelry. If you are not wearing certain fashion names or labels, if you're not wearing at least some of the most expensive wears or jewelry, then you are not socially accepted in some circles. Take a look at what the music and television industry has done to young people generation after generation.

How about the type of vehicle you drive or whether you are slim or overweight; the type of job you have or whether or not you have some sort of college degree? Hey popular culture is what it is and we love it. Without a doubt any type of progress is good and 'is' needed, but what about the damage that is done or the confusion that is created by these things, these ideas?

With a little research, I have found that a good portion of the people who are in need of mental health services or treatment have acquired their condition due to some kind of substance abuse. I have also found that a lot of these same people who have used drugs or are using drugs began using drugs while in junior high or high school. Some of them began using drugs, because they were not accepted in certain social circles or were made to be seen as social outcast, due to their look, style of dress, nationality, etc. Others began using drugs, because they somehow developed the idea that this was the socially acceptable thing to do.

People argue and fight on behalf of religion, music, style of dress, ideas of love or what is morally correct or incorrect. I have sarcastically stated to people in discussions or debates that "you are speaking to me with somebody else's tongue or thinking with somebody else's brain." I mean without a doubt a lot of what we learn comes by way of some idea that someone else has had at some time in the past, and it is very practical to say that with thorough research and experimentation a man could adopt an idea or make that idea 'his own' by taking the time to 'know' whether the idea is realistic for him personally or for others universally; but instead of knowing for sure most of us just tread through life believing what we hear and very rarely take the time to check the validity of anything.

My point is that a lot of us spend a life time trying our hardest to live up to and satisfy some standard, only to fall into depression and develop feelings of inadequacy; thinking that we are not good enough, smart enough, cool enough, pretty or slim enough; thinking that we do not have enough money, a nice enough house or car, all because we are unsuccessful in our attempts to achieve some goal set for us by someone else. Let us revisit the subject of a belief in religion. Most people who hold on to religious beliefs do so, because of fear. We were told when we were young that if we did not believe in God, Allah, etc. that we would burn for eternity in hell. How scary of an idea is that for a young child? Most people who struggle and stress themselves out to keep up with some standard do so, because of the fear of not being accepted. The many standards set for us by our families, our friends or social circles and society as a whole have caused a large number of us to think that to not satisfy these standards means that we are failures. It is this fear of failing or the fear of being ridiculed for failing that keeps us chasing the ghost. What a way to live your life.

Chapter 2

LIVING THE LIE

(Personality vs. Character)

"I never wear anything cheap. Every article of clothing that I buy has to be top of the line. I drive one of the most expensive luxury cars. You know how it is; I have to maintain my image." This same person who made this statement works at a job that pays him just over $9 per hour; that is a little more than $17,000 per year (before taxes). He lives in an apartment where the rent is 500 dollars a month. When you factor in 100 to 200 dollars monthly for utilities, 100 to 200 dollars monthly for food, don't forget the expensive 250 to 350 dollar a month car note and the 200 to maybe 400 dollar a month shopping habit, you have to wonder if this guy has even a penny left at the end of the month?

How many people do you know that are living far beyond their means? I am sure you know quite a few. This may even be you. How do you feel when you have worked so hard in school to receive your bachelor's degree, you find a decent job, make a decent living, yet you still feel empty and unsatisfied. You feel that what you have achieved is not enough, so you go back to school and spend more money chasing degree after degree. We spend so much time trying to keep up that we lose sight of whom we truly are and our entire life becomes a very uncomfortable and dissatisfying lie.

Let us take a turn and approach this from a different angle. People like that which is satisfying to the senses. Your wife or mother bakes cookies and offers you one. The cookie tastes so good that it causes you to say, 'give me another'. An acquaintance of yours walks by and rubs your shoulders and it felt good, so you say to him or her, "hey, do that again". The opposite of that of course is true if the cookie tastes awful or if the acquaintance hurts you when he or she rubs your shoulders. People like that which feels (or tastes) good to the senses. At the risk of sounding redundant, what feels good to us we like. Whatever it is that we like we take an interest in (this is signified by the desire to re-live the satisfying sensation). What we take interest in we are attracted to. Whatever attracts us, we pay attention to. Whatever has or controls your attention, controls YOU. Throughout our lives we have numerous experiences, some good and some 'bad'. The things that we like or enjoy, we indulge in. The things that hurt us or that we don't enjoy, we build a sort of protective barrier against them; and so throughout our life experiences we go through this continual shaping and molding until we create an idea of or about ourselves that is comforting (to us). This created idea is what we present to the world; this is our personality. The problem with this is that WHO we are in presentation to the world and who we are when we are all alone is two different people (or many different people, depending on the individual). What you are experiencing while alone 'in your own counsel' is your true character; that part of you that admits its weaknesses and knows the real reason(s) for all that it does. Now picture this; we go through our daily lives presenting to others what 'we know' is not genuine. How many times have you dreaded the idea of walking into a situation where you knew you would have to laugh at jokes that weren't funny, or keep a smile on your face and all the while knowing that the people with whom you are dealing are themselves phony and back stabbing? How uncomfortable is that? I mean why would you laugh if the joke(s) aren't funny? Why would you put yourself through the turmoil of being around people who you know are phony or backstabbing? In a world full of illusion it can be very hard for a person to know or recognize truth. It is as if our analytical or reasoning faculties have been purposely 'short-circuited'. So now in this present lifetime we are faced with what appears to be an impossible task; that of getting re-acquainted with ourselves. All of your life you've assumed that you knew who you were, what your abilities are or what it is that you want out of life; but the fact is you don't know who you are. This is why you cannot make your relationships work or why you cannot find a career that is satisfying. How many people can 'truly' say that they behave in public, as they behave when they are all alone in their own counsel? Not many. In fact, with the many faces that most of us wear in our attempts to satisfy the many standards that have been set for us by others, who has the time to be themselves?

Chapter 3

FEAR

(Of embarrassment)

A lot of times we wonder what it is about people that causes them to posture themselves in a way that suggests that they are without fear or weakness? What is it that causes a person to so aggressively express that which they themselves know to be untrue? Let us revisit the idea that was introduced in the previous chapter regarding how personality is developed over a period of time based on our experiences.

When a child is born he or she is born in virtue, but as a person travels through the maze of standards established by one's peers and society, his/her thinking becomes vague. In the city of Syracuse (New York) there has been a steady wave of violence; teen violence in particular. Some may attempt to argue that what I am about to say is untrue. My suggestion is that you at least take this into consideration. Think about the message that is communicated through music and/or entertainment, television and movies. It is from these media outlets that standards in fashion, use of language, personal relationships and general behavior are developed in our youth and young adults, in particular. A person who lives in a financially desolate situation and desires to change her condition (based on what she sees on television, what she hears in music or what her friends say "is hot"), but lacks the ability to do so, in an attempt to satisfy the many standards set by peer groups and society, will resort to doing whatever is necessary to satisfy such standards with hopes of avoiding ridicule if unfortunately she fails to succeed. Many people consider many of these standards unachievable. To avoid embarrassment the individual who is incapable of achieving the standard downplays the standard as unimportant or worse, overexerts herself in a way that is detrimental not only to herself, but also to others.

Feelings of inadequacy causes a lot of people to feel weak, unfulfilled, and in some ways, targeted. To avoid the embarrassment related to the exposure of weakness, an individual will lie, steal, cheat, and even resort to violence in the name of self-preservation. What causes a man to argue with his mate about a matter in which he knew he was wrong? What causes a person to debate a subject that they know they have never researched or studied? What is it that causes a student to lash out at his teacher, when the teacher is merely asking the student a question relative to his lesson? What is it that causes one person to feel threatened by the mere presence of another person?   What is it that causes the divide between the younger people and older people in the community?   What is it that creates competition between men in the weight room or women in the beauty parlor? All of these things are created by the idea that one is not satisfying some standard set by someone else.

Consider the high school drop-out rate. The failure of most teenagers to complete high school is more than likely directly related to feelings of pressure stemming from an inability to maintain the status quo in fashion, style, attitude and even test or report card grades. What about the person who acquired the grades necessary for high school graduation, but didn't acquire high enough scores to attend a credible university? There are even some students who consider an education from a community college to be less valuable than an education from a four year school. The idea is that persons who are without an education from credible four-year schools are less likely to succeed than persons with four year degrees.

Imagine what it does to the morale of a person to have feelings of not having done enough. It almost seems as if society is structured in a way that causes people to fail; or at least to cause them to think that they have failed. To live in a society that is built on illusions of value causes one to chase an idea of success that is ever evasive. It would be easy for one to claim that the society in which we live is one that breeds jealousy, hatred, violence and failure by providing people with the dream-stuff for building beautiful air castles, but not with the practical sense, skill and ability required to make any of these dreams materialize. What we have instead is a society built on lies and a people who now unconsciously perpetuate their own destruction; a conglomerate of communities inhabited by a confused people with no real sense of value. What a situation like this creates in those inhabitants is a total disrespect and disregard for others and the community in which they live.

This is not an attempt to put the blame on the society wherein we live; nor is it an attempt to cause the reader to do the same. What it is, is an attempt to empower the reader enough so that he or she may realize that there is no need for fear and their inability to purchase expensive clothing or attract attention doesn't in any way decrease their value.

Chapter 4

SELFISHNESS

(As long as I look & feel good, who cares if you do?)

I remember there was an incident where a young kid who lived next-door to me was the victim of a shooting. I looked out the door and I could see his mother crying. His other family members were pulling up in their vehicles. What I remember most was a statement made by someone standing close by. A woman standing in her doorway one house away from me said, "I'm glad that wasn't my son". What would cause a person to totally disregard the fact that a young person and his family suffered such a tragedy?

Some of us have seen this type of scenario mentioned above on more than one occasion. Some of us have even been that person like the woman one house away from me. Most people are too caught up in their own trials and tribulations to be concerned about another person's problems. As long as we're not having any hard times, who cares if anybody else is. Can this disregard for your fellow man be related to those same feelings of inadequacy as described in the previous chapters?

Let's talk about a subject that we all can relate to, relationships. A man and a woman had been dating for a couple of years. During the course of their relationship the woman has made complaints that the man hasn't been paying enough attention to her. One day the man decides to end what he considered to be a trying relationship. A couple of weeks later, while walking down the street, the man see his ex-girlfriend with a new male friend. Naturally this sighting evoked some former feelings that the man once had for the woman. Later that evening the man decides to call his ex-girlfriend to tell her that he misses her and he wants her back.

Here is the reality: it is not true that the man wants the woman back because he misses her. What is true is that he doesn't want to see any other man with her. So his motives are in fact selfish. Even if this scenario were different, where a couple broke up for a totally different reason, in most cases where one person is claiming to miss the person they've previously dealt with, it is merely a case of one or both individuals selfishly clinging on to the other for the purpose of eliminating their own pain and loneliness. There is hardly ever a time when a person sincerely considers the feelings of the other person when they are attempting to reconcile a situation.

Let us consider another scenario. In a high school setting we have two young ladies; one who is popular and desires more popularity and one who is not so popular. Whenever the unpopular girl is passing through the hallway or sitting in the cafeteria the popular girl makes it her business to make fun of the unpopular girl to generate laughs from her peers. All of this is done by the popular girl in an attempt to increase her popularity and to make herself feel good, without considering the damage that she is doing to the esteem of the unpopular girl. What about the person who sacrifices the career of another for their own personal gain? What about the person who sells drugs to a mother with a total disregard for the small children she has at home; all in the name of the drug dealer's personal progress? What about the leader of a country who sends many to die at war to preserve his family's business interests?

Each of these scenarios are examples of the type of selfishness that eats away at the potential good that exists in every human being. In an attempt to compete in a world where the odds are against most, we tirelessly reach for illusionary gold at the expense of others. Unemployment rates are high, divorce rates are high, crime rates are high, and infant mortality rates are high. People who are sick are unable to afford proper health care and pharmaceutical companies are getting richer every day creating drugs for ailments, which in turn creates other ailments, which will eventually require more drugs, which will create more ailments and all the while no one is getting better.

Most of you will probably never relate this type of behavior to the somewhat unreachable standards established by society and promoted by the media, our peers and our families. Each of us are victims of this social engineering. Even I have to remind myself from time to time that the illusions of value promoted in this society are not valuable at all. Who can, with a good conscience, say that the type of hatred, greed and envy generated via attempts to achieve the status quo is justifiable? What man can justify his beating a woman in his attempt to shield his weaknesses?

What women can justify abusing her child in an attempt to release frustrations stemming from her lack of progress or unhappiness? Even in a less traumatic situation like community conflict over grant money, the principle is still the same. In an attempt to find significance people are continually sacrificing other people without conscience. In jobs of service the people occupying said jobs are no longer applying for these jobs with the intent of helping others, but are applying for these jobs to acquire status.   I'm not sure if there are many politicians who sought public office with the intent of truly bettering his or her community. What then is to become of a nation of soulless people? Vampires or bloodsuckers who feed on the essence of other unsuspecting vampires and bloodsuckers; all that can be expected is more of what has already been.....rot and decay.

Chapter 5

RESPONSIBILITY

(For your thoughts and actions)

What has become funny to me over time is a statement made by people who may have been found guilty of even the smallest thing: "the Devil made me do it". Most of what happens to people is always somebody else's fault. Very seldom do you hear a man claim responsibility for his misfortune. As stated in a previous chapter it is not the intent of the author to blame society for any individual's lack of achievement. While the cause of the problem may be social engineering, our knowledge of the existence of this social engineering empowers us with the ability to bring an end to this mental and emotional enslavement.

Every man or woman who is guilty of damaging his or her personal relationship blames the other person for their relationship's failure. Every drug dealer or burglar, who gets caught, blames society and asserts that a lack of job opportunity is the cause of his trying to "eat fast for free". Every pedophile or child molester blames his or her family and a bad early childhood for an inability to control their hormones or to get a date with someone their own age. Every person found guilty of gang activity, blames the other members of the other gangs for their involvement in questionable activity. Nobody wants to take responsibility for their own actions!

A woman is walking home from work. Every day it takes the woman 30 minutes to get from her job to her house. On her way home she passes an alleyway and she thinks: "if I take the alley I would get home 15 minutes faster than I would if I walked my normal route." Then she also thinks: "but if I take the alleyway something could happen to me". So every day this woman walked home from work passing the alleyway and ignoring the temptation to take the shorter and faster route for fear that danger lurked there. One day she leaves work feeling a little more fatigued than usual. She approaches the alleyway and decides that today she's going to take the faster route. She walks through the alleyway and as she gets halfway through the alley a strange man jumps out from behind a garbage dumpster and rapes her. Here's the question: which person initially had the most control over the potential outcome of this situation? Even though the man should probably be castrated for the crime he committed, the choice to either take the longer or shorter route was ultimately hers. Intuition told her that there would be danger in the alley; nevertheless, for the sake of convenience, she chose to ignore her good conscience and go the shorter, more dangerous route.

How many times have you heard a person say, "even though the relationship was bad and she cheated on me most of the time, 50% of the responsibility was mine, because I chose to be in that relationship?" Nothing happens to any person without that person first exercising the right to choose. Is this point not true even for the unlucky soul who attends a nightclub and after the club closes he walks outside and becomes an innocent victim of a drive-by shooting? "The bullet wasn't intended for him" is what people would say, but the fact is that the bullet was intended for him. Prior to leaving for the club this young man contemplated whether he should go out or stay home. The feeling that he shouldn't go was probably stronger than his desire to be there yet, as time progressed, his desire to go to the club increased and eventually overpowered his good conscience and so fate awaited him.

Some may consider these examples extreme, but in some of our lives these examples all too familiar. The power to choose is the personal property of every single person living on this planet. No one has the right or ability to interfere when an individual is deciding a course of action, except in the case of small children, who in many cases act or behave in accordance to their parent's will.

Let us consider a woman who is a single parent raising three kids on her own. She has an okay job, but it doesn't pay enough for her to cover the cost of her bills and still have money left over for recreation. Knowing that her electricity bill is due, she gambles and decides to splurge a little at the mall thinking that she will find the money from some other source to cover her bill. Soon the bill is past due and she doesn't have the money. At this point she begins to worry and stress and the effects of how she is thinking and feeling is felt by everyone in the house. If she had only made the right choice and paid her bill she would not have been in such a tight situation. As in the aforementioned scenarios the choice and therefore the outcome of the situation was totally in her control and consequently her responsibility.

In principle the idea that every man or woman is responsible for the choices that he or she makes is true for everyone. There is no part of our day where we are not faced with the responsibility of making a choice. Our power to choose allows us the opportunity to shape our circumstances, which means that our lives move according to our dictation. Even in religion people would rather give credit to someone or something that they have never seen even though they have actively (consciously) carried out a deed without noticeable assistance. There is very, very little that happens to anyone that is not the responsibility of the person(s) in question. Everything that transpires in our lives is the direct result of our thoughts and actions. We are the architects or designers of our own fate, the outcome of which is of our doing and our doing alone. No one can ever be the blame for anything that has ever happened in my life; certainly not in my adult life. Every broken bone, every bad relationship, any financial troubles, any conflict of any sort, and any other thing that has happened or will happen to me, good or bad, has happened or will happen as a result of the choices that I have made or will make. While we may not control the cause of every situation, by choosing how or finding better ways to handle adversity we can indeed be instrumental in determining the outcome(s).

Chapter 6

THE KEY: DISCIPLINE

(Avoid repeating experiences)

There is nothing worse than reliving the same horrible experiences over and over again, but for most people this is a common occurrence. Whether we are talking about dead-end jobs, financial struggles, trying relationships, unworthy friendships, or trouble with the law, many people struggle with the problem of reliving undesirable situations. As with any endeavor, to assure success, some sort of strategic or structured plan is required. In order for children to learn, a curriculum must be structured. In order for a business of any kind to succeed a structured format for how a product should be made or sold is needed. Even nature provides its structure for all that lives or moves within it. Structure trains a person to move with precision and such requires discipline. What is it that causes a person to re-do that which is undesirable? It makes me think back to the movie "Groundhog Day" with Bill Murray, where every morning when he woke up he would repeat the same day, seeing the same faces, until he decided one day that each day he would try something different.   The same holds true for the many people throughout society who experience Groundhog Day. The clinical definition for insanity is defined by a person doing the same thing over and over again and each time expecting a different result. A man who has run headfirst into a brick wall would be a fool to get up and run headfirst into that brick wall again. What is wrong with the thinking of a woman who leaves one abusive relationship only to walk straight into another one? What is wrong with the repeat felon who, knowing that selling narcotics or robbing banks landed him in jail the first time, goes right back into the street and attempts to do it again, somehow thinking that this time he will get away? What is wrong with the thinking of the teenager who is picked on every day by his "friends", yet when tomorrow arrives he goes right back to that same group of unworthy friends? What is wrong with the person who continually blows money time and time again, all the while knowing that there are bills that have to be paid; and when the bill is past due he will relive the same stressful moment month after month after month? As mentioned in earlier chapters, throughout our lives we encounter numerous experiences, each of which is to prepare us for the next experience. Each personal relationship may merely be a lesson to prepare us for the <u>one</u> relationship that we could potentially succeed in. The idea is that we learn from the mistakes that we have made in previous situations, so as to avoid repeating the same mistakes in our next or future situation(s). If there are certain characteristics that a woman recognizes in a new or potential mate, which she saw in a mate who abused her in a previous relationship, that woman should have the good sense to walk away from that new person and never look back. Once a person who has served time in jail for committing a crime is released, he, based on past experience(s) should know that he probably needs to try something different. The high school student who feels embarrassed, because he or she has to repeat the same grade should learn from his or her discomfort and make better decisions the second time around, so not to relive the same type of embarrassment again. The unfortunate reality is that most people never learn from their mistakes and so, their lives are a repeat of the same hell over and over again. The key to avoiding these uncomfortable situations is discipline. A man breaks the heart of a woman by ending their relationship. As the woman reflects, she realizes that the relationship wasn't that good for her anyway. One month later the guy comes back and says to the woman, we should give it another try. The first thought that enters the woman's head is a resounding "NO!" but as the man continues to talk, the woman begins to reflect on the good times, her emotions begin to build, and she says, "Okay, we can give it another try". Many of us have been in this situation before, so we know the outcome. More than likely the relationship ended again and for the same reason(s) that it ended before. The mistake made by the woman was ignoring the first response she had in good conscience. If she had only exercised a little discipline and went with her first response she would've never relived such an uncomfortable and unfulfilling situation.

Discipline is the key to a person regaining their personal freedom. There is no other principle more important in this lifetime, for it takes discipline to succeed at anything. To be loyal in a relationship requires discipline. To be prompt for and to be effective in an occupation requires discipline. To be fair and just in all of your dealings, even when others aren't requires discipline. To take a back seat to someone who may be more talented than you, without developing feelings of envy requires discipline. To draw a straight line requires discipline. To control your emotions or anger in the face of adversity requires discipline. To be courteous to others requires discipline. To appreciate and allow evolution to take place in any respect requires discipline. There is nothing in life that escapes the need for structure/discipline. To be in public, as you are when you are all alone requires discipline. The problem with this idea is that to be disciplined requires too much responsibility for the average person. They would much rather, as mentioned in a previous chapter, pawn the responsibility for their life onto someone else.

No man or woman will ever reclaim his or her life, reshape his or her circumstances, improve his or her personal relationships or friendships, changed their financial conditions, maintain good mental and physical health, or find happiness without first acquiring the required discipline needed to achieve any of the above or any of the many things not mentioned here. It is time that we as individuals stand up and take responsibility for ourselves and our direction. Discipline is the key.

Chapter 7

WHO AM I

(What is my real value?)

Who am I? This is the question of a lifetime, for if we all knew the answer none of us would have any trouble facing our "problems". I have asked many people over the years the question "who are you?" What is interesting is that almost none of the people of whom I've asked this question had an answer. How is that? Most of the time when this question is asked the person responding answers by explaining, "what they are" and not "who they are". I guess with trying to satisfy so many standards established by or within society, it is very easy for a person to lose sight of who they really are. Most people identify themselves with the occupation they have or by the things they possess. Instead of finding that thing about themselves that makes them valuable they validate themselves by what they own or by the people with whom they associate. A person who is known for his great ability in the game of basketball floats into oblivion once his basketball career is over, because as far as he knows, this was the one thing of value that he possessed. This assumed value he received via the standards established within society. Unfortunately for him, once his value has diminished in the eyes of society, it has also simultaneously diminished within him. Absent basketball, who would've ever known him anyway?

There are many people who seek this type of validation from sources outside of themselves. If you are good at basketball or if you desire to be good at basketball, do it because you want to be good or because you love the game of basketball and not because of the status and/or reputation that you think you will acquire as a result of being good at playing basketball. To practice and improve your skill at basketball for the purpose of notoriety will only prove to be disappointing in the end, for there are certain requirements to qualify and play at the collegiate or professional level. Most people who play basketball will never reach said levels, but the person who loves to play basketball will continue to play regardless of the recognition that he or she receives.

In principle, the same applies to any person in any profession. A lawyer loses his job and his world crumbles. A guy is rejected by his friends and his feelings of personal value disappear. A woman who was once poor marries a wealthy man. One day the man files for divorce and because of the prenuptial agreement the woman leaves in the same condition that she was in when she arrived: poor. This is a tragic situation for the woman, because not only did she not use the time wisely by figuring out a way to invest in herself, but most of her time was spent bragging to her family and friends about how she didn't have to work and how her man took care of her. She validated herself by her husband's occupation and successes, none of which she could receive credit for. This is the end of the world for her, because her husband was her savior and now she is right back in the type of situation that she dreads the most.

Sit back and think for a moment: who would you be absent your occupation, personal possessions, or social affiliations acquire as a result of the two things previously mentioned? You wouldn't be the basketball player; you wouldn't be the lawyer; you wouldn't be the politician; you wouldn't be the notorious drug dealer; you wouldn't be the class bully; you wouldn't be the movie star; you wouldn't be the singer or rap star; you wouldn't be the professor or the judge or the Executive Director; you wouldn't be the fire man or the policeman; you wouldn't be the factory worker, the doctor, the psychologist, the contractor, the Minister. You wouldn't have the mansion or the expensive car or the expensive clothing. You wouldn't attract the same friends or associates; you wouldn't attract the same fame and notoriety; so, who would you be?

Believe it or not, a lot of people would answer by saying that they would be nobody. This is because through conditioning their ideas about what is truly valuable are a little off. What about the quiet, respectful, tranquil individual whom you experience every day when you are all alone and none of these external illusions of value are around to influence you? For a woman no makeup is required. She could wear rollers and a face mask if she wants to. She doesn't have to wear fancy clothes or be concerned about whether her shoes match her outfit. She doesn't have to watch how she eats and can eat like a pig without fear of being judged. For a man there is no posturing of himself so not to appear weak to others.   He can listen to love songs or watch girly movies without being labeled as a softy by his peers.   Most importantly, both men and women can be honest with themselves while reflecting on past events in their lives and choosing more productive ways to conduct themselves when encountering experiences in the future. A person of good character doesn't have to pretend in order to be accepted. Such an individual is truly honest with himself about his weaknesses and he works continuously to correct them; not to satisfy others, but to satisfy himself. He will not lie to himself when he knows that he is wrong.   She will not exaggerate the truth, but will instead tell it like it is regardless of the benefits or repercussions. She is courteous and therefore will never sacrifice another person for her own personal gain or comfort. She will not speak with a forked tongue, gossiping or destroying another person's reputation, so to better position herself in the eyes of her audience.

A man or woman of character does the due diligence to make himself or herself better and thereby enable themselves to contribute to the perfection of another man's or woman's character. A man or woman of character walks and talks with dignity and respect; their movement and speech are methodical and deliberate. They are fair dealing and will never take that which is not rightfully theirs. A man or woman of character will never seek to gain at another's expense. A man or woman of character will admit their wrong in the name of peace and progress. A man or woman of character will never allow pride or personality to interfere with and/or confuse a situation. A man or woman of character never needs pride, for they understand that pride is a defense mechanism for the weak. A man or woman of character never uses personality to shield or hide weakness. A man or woman of character will always be true to who they are, for they understand that character is the skeletal structure or frame-work within that causes man and woman to maintain an upright position in mind and spirit and to always remain upon the square in all of their dealings.

With all that has been said, ask yourself: are you a man or woman of character?

BOOK II

NOW

NOW

BY

KHALID EL BEY

DEYEL PUBLISHING COMPANY

217 WEST KENNEDY STREET,
SYRACUSE, NEW YORK [13205]

CREATIVE RESEARCH SOCIETY

SYRACUSE, NEW YORK

PREFACE

An old Buddhist teaching states that "the meeting of Heaven (time) and Earth (space) gives birth to the realm   of   illusion."

The interface of polar opposites, simply put, gives rise to what we perceive as manifest reality. Humanity's self-realization/self-awareness developed as a result of the need for the inner Self to gather and process incoming information from the outside world, and this gave rise to the ego, whose true purpose is to interface with the outside world and to bring the resulting experience to the attention of the   hidden   or   internal   Self. Khalid Bey's work demonstrates the true source of human suffering: the fact that we have reversed the roles of the inner Self and the ego. We have "fallen asleep" and allowed the ego to run the show, to the point that we now erroneously believe we ARE the ego, hence we are our experiences. We begin to then live within in artificial constructs of fatalism and uncertainty, wherein we take on the characteristics of these realms, believing our circumstances are either forever fixed or hopelessly nebulous. Either condition renders the sufferer inconstant and paralyzed, and unable to change their conditions.

Between Heaven and Earth is a third position: Man.

An old Moorish proverb states: "there is no Good that does not come with its admixture of evil, yet God always provides us with the means of throwing off the evil from the Good." We have become so comfortable in the hells of Past and Future and the limited liability of allowing the ego to lead our existence, that the mere idea of leaving either Past or Future and coming to the real world where the inner Self resides is literally a notion that we directly relate to physical death; and in a very real sense this is not far from the truth.

The alchemical admonition "solve et coagula" teaches us that the fixed state of the ego must be made malleable, and this is a kind of death, and is affected by using the Will/Energy to direct the projection of the ego inwards towards the inner Self; away from the Past and the Future and towards the NOW.

"NOW" is an unfamiliar, terrifying, yet exciting place to be. Khalid Bey challenges the reader to "go where no man (the reader) has gone before." "NOW" compels you to die; to murder (sublimate) the ego and pride, and to destroy the comfortable prisons it has constructed; Now compels us to abandon illusion and explore the real world. Be certain that if you follow Mr. Bey's course of action YOU WILL DIE; but in reality the fear of death is really the fear of the meeting with the inner Self.

-   *Sharif Anael Bey*

INTRODUCTION

This very moment where you are right now is the most important moment of your life. It holds the solution or the key to all of your problems and/or concerns. There is not a more opportune moment in time for you to lay a foundation towards a more productive, purposeful and fulfilling life.

There are many of us who suffer silently day in and day out. Dissatisfaction with the decisions and/or actions of our past and fear of the uncertainty of tomorrow increases our stress levels to the point of high blood pressure, cardiac arrest, aneurysms, strokes, etc. Every single person on this planet wants and deserves a peaceful and productive existence. We search high and low for opportunity, hoping to find an answer or a solution somewhere out there in the world, but often with very little to no success. Such a dilemma creates in the average person confusion resulting in intellectual and emotional handicaps so severe, that the persons in question self-destructs, sometimes purposefully. Our lack of understanding about life, our preoccupation with the superficial, our inability remain consistently attentive allows for our lives to spin hopelessly out of control leading to repeat dissatisfaction and despair. In more than half of the cases alcoholism and drug abuse becomes the escape.

This work is intended to be used as a guide for repairing one's life; to provide the reader the tools necessary for the reconstruction of their thinking. My suggestion is that you read this book more than once and refer to this book in times of confusion. In each chapter I attempt to provide proof to the reader of certain ideas or principles that may assist them in their efforts towards self-improvement. To empower an individual to be self sufficient is one of the greatest gifts you could give, leading them to a feeling of freedom never before experienced.

- *KEB*

Part One

POLARITY

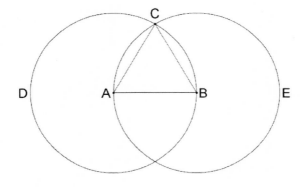

The first problem of Euclid, which states that on any given straight line, an equilateral triangle can be formed, leads to the understanding that for everything that exists there is an opposite. For example, up and down, left and right, inside and outside, male and female, darkness and light, truth and falsehood, God and the Devil, powerful and weak, wide and narrow, fast and slow, etc. Every force in existence has an opposite or receiver of said force. When one thinks of opposites what naturally comes to mind is the idea of two separate things; but even within a single object opposing natures or polarity can be found.

One example to consider is this: when a child is born he receives a total of 46 chromosomes: 23 come from the father and 23 come from the father's opposite (the mother). The child, as a single being, embodies an equal amount of chromosomes from each parent. Another example to consider is the fact that a human being possesses a mind, the opposite of which could be said to be a physical body. A house or similar structure clearly displays polarity having an interior and exterior. Within our bodies are red blood cells that have the primary function of supplying oxygen to all body tissue and organs, and (opposite in its character to oxygen) carbon dioxide is the waste that is the result of the body's metabolism, which eventually exits the body. White blood cells help combat infection(s). Some white blood cells act as scavengers by engulfing foreign particles (such as bacteria) and destroying them. In each example, opposing natures or behaviors are displayed: red blood cells, which express a creative behavior versus white blood cells, which demonstrates a destructive behavior; also oxygen which enters versus carbon dioxide, which exits.

When considering the idea of polarity what must be realized is that for every idea or object, there is an opposing idea or object providing the former balance. Within the universe there exists what should be the most obvious, but is probably the most unobvious polarity: space or an apparent nothingness, and the objects, which occupy said space or nothingness. Consider this: the planet Jupiter due to its size and magnetic power acts as an anchor to the Sun. There exists a tug-of-war between the Sun and Jupiter that keeps the planets between them in order. In other words, the gravitational pull between the two larger planetary bodies, each at opposite ends in this example help the smaller planetary bodies maintain a relatively consistent, balanced orbit. Our Sun according to science is reportedly the tail end of an explosion initiated at some other point in space billions of miles away. In biblical lore, polarity is displayed by the changing of the names of Abram to Abraham and Jacob to Israel. Abram to Abraham being the spirit incarnating, while Jacob to Israel being its ascension from the gross (matter) to the most pure (spirit).

If we were to take a look at two of the three supernal elements, fire and water (air being the third), one would not only notice that each is the opposite of the other, but also that within each of these two elements there exist the potential for creation and destruction.   The initial Life impulse with its very first movement creates a 'pocket of air or archetypal container', which is clearly the resulting opposite (effect) of its movement.

Polarity is defined as: [*Physics*] – *1a. the property or characteristic that produces unequal physical effects at different points in a body or system, as (with)   a   magnate   or   storage   battery.* (Dictionary.com)   Translation: the   physical characteristics (or appearance) or make-up or behavior of a thing or idea, which establishes exact differences or effects, from the object or idea to which it is being compared. (I'm not sure if that translation was any simpler.)

An understanding of polarity or opposing forces is the <u>beginning</u> of the understanding of all of creation.   If we use for example a fairly recognizable or simple situation, such as a desire to eat caused superficially by stomach growling and hunger pains, one could recognize cause and effect. This same principle applies to every part of existence, for there is (arguably) no effect without cause.   Every human emotion has an opposing emotion, which works to offset the former. This of course is a very important factor for one who attempts the sometimes-impossible discipline of smiling in the face of adversity.   In chemistry every element has an opposing element, just as in mundane (physical) life there is the ever appearance of polarity: opposing political parties; the sky and the earth; movable and immovable objects, etc. Take a moment to observe all around and witness the existence of opposites everywhere and in everything.

Molecular Polarity
An Explanation

While reading this section, do your best to remain attentive and stay with me, for if you haven't already, you will catch on.

Polarity is a physical property (or appearance of difference[s]) of or between compounds, objects, etc., which relates other physical properties such as melting and boiling points, solubility, and intermolecular interactions between molecules. The properties mentioned, i.e. melting points, solubility, intermolecular interactions, simply imply a change or transformation happening to the object(s) in question. An example would be ice, which is solid in characteristic, melting or changing to into liquid once placed in a warmer climate. Relationship (comparison/correspondence) is therefore established between the solid ice and the climate, and between the ice and water. For the most part, there is a direct relation between the polarity of a molecule and number and types of polar or non-polar (referred to as covalent) bonds which are present. Covalent (or non-polar) bonding is when two atoms share two electrons. The two electrons shared by the atoms are attracted to the nucleus of both atoms. Neither atom completely loses or gains electrons as in ionic bonding. In Non-polar bonds there is <u>an equal sharing</u> of electrons; balance therefore is the result. Polar bonding is when there is an <u>unequal</u> sharing of electrons, causing domination of one (extreme) 'force' or in this case, the domination of one electron over the other. If one was to have a scale and on one side placed one stone and on the other side placed two stones of equal size and mass to the first (stone), an understanding of Polar bonding would be received. In a simpler explanation: Polar bonding is when too much energy is given in one direction or to one extreme, thereby causing the neglect of the opposite extreme and creating an imbalance. Another example: If the Sun's gravitational pull increased to the point where it overpowered Jupiter, the smaller planets in between would move out of orbit, eventually crashing and burning on the Sun. Non-polar bonding is when there is an equal distribution of energy in both directions; **neither extreme is overpowered nor neglected and so balance is maintained.** This means that the balance or imbalance is determined by the number of Non-polar bonds there are in a body or system in comparison to the number of Polar bonds in that same body or system. Put simply, balance and equilibrium in ones circumstances (or the lack thereof) is determined by the number of non-polar situations there are compared to the number of polar situations there are in said circumstances.

In life most of us are obligated by circumstance(s) to find work or a career to enable us to take care of ourselves, our families and other responsibilities. As commonly found in most situations, a majority of the energy that one has tends to be focused in <u>one</u> of the two directions. This 'polar bonding' causes an imbalance, resulting in stress, worry, dissatisfaction, disruption and failure in the opposite area that is receiving less energy.

In politics and government too much of a (monetary) focus on the war in Iraq and Afghanistan and/or the outsourcing of jobs to compete in the global economy had caused a recession here in the United States. Where the mind is concerned, too much energy or focus on negatives, such as fear of failure and disappointment, causes one to neglect and therefore **paralyze** the opposite emotional responses of courage and satisfaction.

Conclusion

One would wonder about the <u>reason</u> or purpose for an opposing force; an idea that has been known and spoken about by many more qualified than I on the subject. The idea of polarity existing in all things or in all of Life creates for many the most confusing and contradicting ideas and circumstances. This very 'necessary' contradiction though, is the mechanism needed (and used knowingly and/or unknowingly) to validate Life. This reality is displayed by the explanation of ratio and proportion in Mathematics or by the manifestation of 'bad' in the midst of 'good'. One way to display the 'need' or value for contradiction is to ask yourself 'how would one know good, were it not for bad?' 'How could one accurately categorize the idea of a Devil, were there not an idea of a 'God' to compare him or her to?'

Every physical thing that exists is identified and categorized by its physical characteristics *being compared* to another object's physical characteristics. I must though repeat one fact, so to forever embed it into the reader's memory: All objects (or ideas) which appear separate from other objects (or ideas) are in fact 'whole' themselves and therefore dual in nature. Birth and death though appearing to be contradicting or separate events are in fact the same phenomenon: Life. It is a repeated entrance into and exit out of a 'looping' or continuum; and it is this 'continuum' or world of events, definition and finality into which Life chaotically leaps for no other apparent purpose, except to validate its own existence. Through polarity, the universe and all that exist within it and without it is noticed, contradicted, established and/or validated; for absent such contradictions leading to validation, Life and all that is the result of Life would be naught.

Part Two

SHADOW TIME

The idea of home has become, for me, a very interesting concept. When one contemplates 'home' what immediately comes to mind is the house or apartment within which one resides. In addition to the aforementioned, when considering the concept of home one also thinks of a place to which one would always return; a place where comfort and security could be found; where one's family and/or loved ones dwell.

For many, the idea of home at times is broader in context. 'Home' could refer to a town, city, state, or even one's native country. There are even some cases where the concept of home might not apply to any of the above mentioned locales, but instead simply refers to specific surroundings, i.e. persons or a familiar environment. When examined further, the idea of home becomes less tangible and more abstract. The idea of home suggests for most people, stability. Yet the general idea of home (stability) falls short when a person relocates or changes her residence. In many cases most people do not remain in the same house, apartment, or even the exact same area (code) of their birth; so it may be argued that a person throughout the course of her life has many homes; unless it could be better argued that home might imply something altogether totally different.

Think about this for a moment; imagine what it would be like if your entire memory failed. If an individual's memory failed completely, he would not recognize his own thumb let alone his house or neighborhood. It could be argued that all we are or all that we claim to be is recorded or programmed into our memory. Our ideas of comfort and security; our ability to recognize our house, neighborhood, even our family, depends 'totally' on the 'compartment' of mind that houses the memory. Is it possible that what one identifies as home is in fact a memory of a specific feeling (comfort, security, etc.)? Clearly one's true home, if such an idea could be coined, is not necessarily characterized by the physical structure that one dwells in for any particular amount of time; for it appears that this 'sense of home' could be established where ever one chooses to dwell.

I would argue that no matter one's surroundings; no matter the number of people living with an individual within the same structure (house); no matter the number of physical structures (houses) one has occupied; said individual(s) lives alone in his/her own home/world (mind). A person's external behavior is a reflection of his thoughts. How one communicates, dresses, or acts in general is the result of the 'mind stuff' that he experiences all unto himself. Despite what might be assumed regarding the everyday life of any particular person, no person has ever had any 'physical' visitors, nor will he ever have such visitors in his true home, or his true place of comfort and security (his head/mind).

Each and every one of us resides in a place that is peopled by ghost. What I mean by this is that all that we are and all that we know is the result of our memories; those intangible, fluffy, less than crystallized images housed in the shadows. This is the place where each person on this planet resides. It is here where one lives out her life in its entirety, ALONE; fighting battles, some won, some lost, real or imagined, to her benefit or detriment.

Chapter one discussed polarity or the fact that with everything that exists there is an opposite. Chapter one further discussed the need to avoid extremes; for to lean too far towards one extreme would result in the neglect of the opposite (extreme). Man's preoccupation with his external world has caused him to neglect his not so obvious mental world. Think about this for a moment: if most or all that is your external life is the result of your internal life/mind/thoughts, then understandably a life that neglects the mind is a life of disappointment and disaster. For the person who neglects the mind or for those who cause damaged to the brain due to the bad habits of smoking, drinking, etc., it must be realize that though appearing to be separate, these polar opposites (mind & external life) correspond with each other; they are connect. The same applies to the builder of 'air castles 'or persons who dreams much, but builds or produces very little (externally). All of his time is spent in his mind imagining accomplishments; accomplishments which he never physically attempts to achieve. Ultimately, the neglect of either one will result in the destruction of the other. As I stated earlier, home is an interesting concept. People reside in the shadows, but believe otherwise; and it is their preoccupation with the "otherwise", that results in an inability to recognize the need for light (learning) amidst the shadows.

My intent in this chapter is to demonstrate the reality that though a man's life appears to play itself out in the third dimension (physical world), his outward behavior is a mere dramatization of what he thinks. Everyday there are persons who struggle to establish themselves or find their place in the scheme of things, but fail to make <u>any investment</u> at all into their mental life (any potentially progressive investments that is). Instead what's collected in the mind of the individual is all of the junk; the worry, stress and similar poisons which further inhibit the individual's potential for progress; ultimately causing one's life to *seem* disappointing and unfulfilled; even unbearable. To me, information is money, for the more you know (in this society) the more valuable you are. Every new idea, every new thing learned has an undeterminable value. Imagine that you invested as much time and energy into your thinking, as you do your finances and other possessions; how well off would you be?

Part three

TIME TRAVEL

In the next two chapters I am going to discuss what I realized to be two of the greatest hindrances of man. His first hindrance is his past.

Time and again each of us as human beings spend moments of our life dissatisfied. For some, the time spent dissatisfied is only for a moment; but for others, dissatisfaction is felt without end. Feelings of dissatisfaction and disappointment are, in many cases, the result of regret felt for choices made in our past. Regularly, a woman beats herself up for exhibiting an unproductive behavior or for choosing an action that failed to produce an outcome she desired. So many of us are plagued with feelings of disappointment and dissatisfaction for the very same reasons, and so our inability to let go of yesterday or our dissatisfaction with choices made yesterday becomes one of our greatest obstacles.

A man reflects on a disruption in his personal relationship that had taken place a year into his past. Amazingly, he travels back into time (memory) and re-experiences the pain and disappointment relative to that moment; so much so, that he actually **re-invokes** former feelings associated with the past experience into his present experience. As a result, said (past) experience is <u>relived</u> all over again as if it had 'just happened' in the (present) moment. The above-mentioned spectacular(s) are performed by so many every single day. Who says that a man can't time travel? Unfortunately, for whatever reason human beings struggle with the idea that there are no do-overs; that whatever has happened yesterday has passed into oblivion; and our preoccupation with moments in our past inhibits our ability to move forward. Take for example the idea of a man who is unemployed and who is searching for employment opportunities. In his immediate past the quest for employment bore no fruit; naturally he grew dissatisfied, because of his lack of success. As the days go by the search for employment appears bleak. His self-confidence diminishes and eventually, he stops looking. After about a week of relaxation he decides to give it another go, only this time after getting dressed and collecting his resume he gets to the door, but never exits. Unfortunately his thoughts about his past failures made him apprehensive about going out and asking for work.

He began to think "why even bother, I'm not going to get hired anyway". Ultimately, his confronting his circumstances with apprehension, caused by his fear of failing resulted in the evitable. Being afraid of failure led him to avoid the opportunity to fail by not applying for the job in the first place, which in the end became his failure after all. In this instance, he is experiencing the disappointment of rejection by his own hand. 'He' rejected himself in order to avoid experiencing rejection that he assumed and feared was coming from someone else, whom he has never even had the pleasure of meeting.

A woman meets a man and becomes very excited about the potential of a new relationship. He is intelligent, attractive, industrious, and possesses so many other qualities that a woman desires in a potential mate. Though this new guy has all of these great qualities to his credit, the woman never allows herself to totally commit. She has experienced so much disappointment in her past personal relationships, that she is terrified of reliving similar circumstances. This fear of disappointment in love causes her to approach her new potential relationship with apprehension. What she does not know is that this new guy senses her apprehension and in turn becomes apprehensive himself. Ladies and gentlemen this is the classic failure of a relationship. By her being apprehensive, her new boyfriend who recognizes her apprehension becomes apprehensive and a wedge is established between the two. Ultimately, the relationship is doomed from the start and what was most feared by the woman is assured (another failed relationship). If my preoccupation with the infidelity of my past mate(s) causes me to not trust the sincerity of present or future mates, I will never allow myself the opportunity to experience a truly fulfilling relationship for fear that it will fail. My behavior would do no more than teleport past feelings associated with past circumstances into the present. If for every step a man took forward he followed that forward step with two steps backwards, where would he end up? Disappointment due to a lack of progress is assured.

It is unfortunate that so many of us struggle with our pasts decisions and/or experiences, but what must be understood is that forward movement will continue to be a struggle for as long as we expend countless energy traveling into yesterday. No person on this planet can travel due North with absolute accuracy, while facing (and in most cases, traveling) due south. If the message in part one of this book clarified nothing else, it made clear that too much focus to one extreme (i.e. the past) causes the neglect and eventual destruction of the opposite extreme.

Part Four

THERE IS NO TOMORROW

The previous chapter discussed one of the two greatest hindrances to man; that being his preoccupation with his past. Another of Man's greatest hindrances is his preoccupation with his future.

I know that reading the above statement will cause many to disagree with the idea of one's preoccupation with tomorrow hindering his progress. I only asked that before allowing your mind to shut off or before disagreeing, you at least give due consideration to what I am about to say.

While the idea of one's past hindering his progress might be easily understood, the idea that one's concern about his future might create for him a fate similar to the aforementioned understandably is puzzling to some; but many of us experience a great amount of fear and stress when contemplating our future. In fact, if you compile the uncertainty of tomorrow with our constant struggles to make definite decisions, my reasoning might become clearer. Think about some of the examples mentioned in the previous chapter. The man who experienced failure in his previous attempts to find an occupation gave up in the end, due to the <u>assumption</u> (prediction) that he would not succeed at finding a job. His choice to no longer look for a job was based on his expected failure (future tense). His fears associated with a potential <u>future outcome</u> caused him to not make an effort in the moment. This brings us to the position that I am presenting to you, and that is that one of the greatest causes of disappointment and, which ultimately leads to failure is <u>expectation</u>, or more particularly, hope absent effort. Either a person assumes the worse as with the unemployed gentlemen, or something that one might have been expecting does not come into fruition. In both cases the individual(s) concerned will usually feel disappointed and/or dissatisfied with the outcome(s). These persons tend to feel defeated, which leads to feelings of inadequacy, self-doubt, and ultimately their own undoing.

Naturally you might be thinking "well, what do we do, not plan for our future?" No, that is not what I am saying. What comes under question is <u>the amount of value you place on the thing expected</u>. If you are a person who validates yourself by the things you possess, by the people with whom you associate, or by your "accomplishments", then your dissatisfaction is understood. Should one or more of these things not pan out, the person in question begins to question their significance and their value. On the contrary, if you do not place value on your possessions, your associates, your accomplishments, etc., losing any of these things will have very little (negative) effect on you. (Read Book I, **the Key to Character** for a further discussion about personal significance) People are so afraid of tomorrow's disappointment that they walk, speak, and even breathe with apprehension. Consider the woman mentioned in the previous chapter. She had experienced so much disappointment in her past personal relationships, that she never allowed herself to commit herself 100% to her new relationship, for fear of experiencing a similar disappointment. As you can see many of us even fear the expected (future) loss, disappointment, ridicule, embarrassment, etc., associated with our past experiences. This idea reminds me of a quote that I often make: "many of us spend so much of our time and energy trying not to die, that we forget to live." People, I assure you that a life lived with apprehension is not a life at all.

All of us have been taught ideas of what constitutes wins and losses. Our desire(s) to win, coupled with our desire(s) to avoid loss are a major cause of the stress experienced by each of us daily. Not knowing what tomorrow has in store for us drives us to indulge in activities (alcohol, drugs, promiscuity, etc.) or to exhibit behavior (especially frustration and vulnerability) that assures no more than our absolute destruction. As mentioned in an earlier chapter, there are no do-overs. Yesterday is gone and you cannot get it back; let it rest. You would do yourself a great service by simply realizing the value of or lesson associated with a given past experience, and as a result, improve your behavior/choices/etc., so to avoid repeating such undesirable circumstances as you continue to live your life. What you must also understand is that there is in fact <u>no</u> tomorrow. Think about it; when you arrive to tomorrow, it'll be today. When you arrive to next week, it'll be this week and the next minute will be this minute and next year will be this year. The truth is you never 'really' reach or even witness a 'tomorrow'. Tomorrow is a concept at best that attempts to capture the idea of 'a distance or a point in space/time; which is essentially no different, nor any less local than where you are currently sitting or standing right now. Here's a test: remain where you are right now for 24 hours. Outside of increasing muscle fatigue and hunger pains or the Earth spinning on its axis causing the Sun to appear to disappear, make a note of what about 'the day itself' actually changes (specifically to a 'tomorrow'). Better yet, just explain to anyone what constitutes tomorrow. Good luck.

How is it that we have become so disillusioned that we live in fear of an idea that never materializes? Our fears of not achieving our goals, dreams, wishes, etc, inhibit us all in every way imaginable. This tendency to self-destruct has become a common behavior of each of us. Do I need to reiterate the clinical definition of insanity? Maybe so.

The clinical definition of insanity is to repeat the same thing over and over again, each time expecting a different result.

Throughout the entirety of each and every one of our lives, we have made plans repeatedly. Very, very seldom has ANY of our plans EVER turned out exactly the way that we had envisioned. Nevertheless, each and every one of us acts shocked and is devastated when our efforts fail to produce the desired outcome. So, we continue to plan, fail, and stress. How insane are you?

At what point do we realize that we need to plan with elasticity; to not be attached to any particular desired outcome, but instead appreciate the outcomes that we do experience? Knowing that very little has ever turned out exactly the way you've expected, why would you expect your next plan to produce at any greater level of accuracy? I am not saying that prediction is impossible; only that most of us aren't any good at predicting outcomes. This scenario reveals one uncomfortable truth: that your disappointment and unfortunate undoing is self-inflicted.

Part Five

NOW

"In a right angled triangle: the square of the hypotenuse is equal to the sum of the squares of the other two sides."

- Pythagorean Theorem

You might ask: 'What was the purpose of this Author's proof of extremes; particularly yesterday and tomorrow?'

My intent is to prove to the reader one ever escaping (apparently hidden) reality; that the key to solving the riddle of extremes resides in the middle.

Our preoccupations with yesterday and tomorrow causes each of us to neglect the most important and best part, TODAY. Our continual departure from the NOW into shadow time (past/future) leaves absolutely little to no focus on the moment, resulting in stagnation; for it is in the NOW, via of our choices and actions that we simultaneously lay out our history, which in turn become our foundation for the future. If there is no decision and no action in the NOW, there will be no traces of yesterday and so no ground work performed to assure our tomorrow.

There are many areas of our life where the principle of equilibrium is demonstrated; where the middle road has proven to be the best path. For example: the sum total and so the best part of a Man and a Woman is the offspring. Communication sets in the 'middle ground' between opposite-equals. When communication fails, imbalance (polarity) is the result. Love, dwelling in the center of a Man and a Woman in a relationship is the connection or the tie that binds; for absent the principle of love, all is in disarray. The 'hand-shake' too lies in the middle of two people symbolizing a compromise or shared vision; a common ground. The conscious mind lies in the in-between of internal and external life; so understandably to be unaware in the moment is to deny one the opportunity to invest in him/herself.

There are countless examples of the need for balance and equilibrium between opposites; two of the most obvious examples of extremes being war and peace; where understanding and tolerance is the solution.

Spend a minute contemplating the moment. Try your best not to think about what happened in each second that has already passed you by. Do not think about yesterday and do not think about what you have to do in the next hour; just stay HERE. Remain attentive to ever word you read without allowing your mind to wander. Stay with me; only 30 more seconds remaining; there is nothing else to consider except these words that you are reading right NOW. NOW; see, that is the idea; to stay in the NOW. Ok, stop and answer this: while focusing on the above message did anything else come to mind? Did you feel any stress or worry? Did you feel anything at all? If you were able to remain in the moment you would not have experienced any of the above feelings. Feelings of worry, stress, dissatisfaction, etc, are directly related to (negative) thoughts about our past and future. A better control over *'where we place our **attention**'* will relieve us of so many of the negative emotions we are accustomed to experiencing. Practice the above test enough and I assure you that it will become second nature.

The ideas expressed in this small book will prove to be invaluable to the person(s) seeking to change their lives. It is the **choices** we make that help to shape our circumstances. If we want different circumstances, we have to begin to *choose differently*. While the contrast or contradictions or polarity described in this book creates, for each and every one of us, challenges; such challenges or conflict(s) are the sculptors' tools used to carve out the intricacies of one's thinking, one's appearance and the differing details of one's life. These conflicts provide the controversy, losses, confusion and triumphs that serve as those very necessary lessons that are critical to our development as Human Beings. These spaces or extremes of loss and victory are not where we are to remain; but it is instead in the in-between or the compromise of these extremes where we will find the equilibrium and balance or the peace and harmony that we so desperately need. There is nobody home, but you. You and you alone have to power to improve your circumstances, and so, your life. All you have to do is realize this:

'In order to change your world, all you would have to do is change your mind.'

NOW

BOOK III

Love Under Will

Love Under Will

By

Khalid El Bey

To everyone who has ever struggled to find
the Holy Grail.

Preface

The subject of personal relationships is undoubtedly one of the most challenging that anyone of us has ever had to face. Our constant efforts towards perfection are consistently met by frustration and despair. Throughout times immemorable authors have taken a shot at providing some sort of solution to the mystery of love. Unfortunately, despite those great and noble efforts the struggle to discover the Holy Grail persists. Does this suggest that the many of the past who have attempted to articulate or reveal said mystery has failed? Definitely not; contrarily I would argue that many of us over the years have not prepared ourselves to see and/or receive what may be true. This small book is yet one more attempt to assist in the effort to eliminate delusion. It is my hope that the reader finds the content enlightening and invigorating.

THE MISCONCEPTION

There exists in life a treasure, so valuable, so desirable, yet so evasive, that it is sought by every single human being on Earth. It is a treasure more precious than gold or money, more precious than fame and prestige, and sometimes more precious than even family. You ask yourself, what could be so desirable to all, consciously or not, that would cause those things possessing a noticeably tangible value, to lose said value in the face of this ever evasive, less tangible treasure? What is it that despite one's will to resist causes a person to behave in a way that might prove to be detrimental to all that he holds dear?

Obviously by the title of this book the reader(s) can discern that the subject matter or the treasure about which I am speaking is Love.

There have been many who deemed themselves experts on this subject, and who have attempted to provide the struggling populace with a solution to a 'problem', that even they themselves have not accurately identified. It has become characteristic in American society for sure, to treat symptoms and thereby provide the illusion of improved health, wealth, etc.; yet an inability to cure or the choice to ignore the causes of our dis-ease assures us a return to the most undesirable of conditions. This constant return to undesirable conditions causes us to further add to our misery via the assumption of failure; a failure that each and every one of us has witnessed first-hand so many times throughout our past.

Love, is the most promoted idea in every aspect of life, period. We hear about or witness expressions of Love on television, in movies, music, religion, politics and government, and the list goes on. How is it that our most promoted and most desired treasure is simultaneously our greatest cause of disappointment and despair? As with all matters of science (and yes, believe it or not, this may very well qualify as a science), we should approach this matter first by observing, identifying and defining the problem.

Observation: most people fail at <u>establishing</u> Love.

Problem: most people have absolutely no idea about what Love is.

For just about every person the idea of Love is as promoted in soap operas and R&B music. It is due to the fact that Love is so broadly and so wrongfully defined that continual failure is experienced by those in search of it.

For generations Love has been defined as a 'funny feeling in the pit of our stomachs'. It has been characterized by the exhibiting of behavior that is very similar to a person controlled by an addiction (alcohol, drugs, etc.). This misconception of Love has been and continues to be the cause of an array of drastically devastating outcomes; from domestic violence, street conflict, conflict amongst teens and adults alike to conflicts that in many cases has led or leads to rape, robbery, murder and other heinous crimes. Families, careers, reputations, fortunes, opportunities for progress, good mental & physical health, homes, children, lifestyles and many other things that one might consider valuable has been lost as a result of our misunderstanding and the resulting mishandling of Love. How could something so precious cause Man to be so destructive?

Could it be that it is our misunderstanding of the principle of Love that is the cause of our woes? Often we may come across that which looks like Love, smells like Love, and even tastes like Love, but what unfortunately may not be (Love) after all.

It could very well be that our failure to effectively identify what Love is in fact, keeps us chasing sensational ideas of perfection; ideas that have never even crystallized in our minds. Crystallization of course is nearly impossible absent any real knowledge of what love is. Understandably, attempts to locate that which has not been accurately identified may be futile. A very, very simple example: we are sitting in a kitchen and I ask you to pass me 'that' fork. You go and pick up a fork, bring it back to me and I say, 'No, not that fork'. You go to pick up another fork, bring it to me and I say, 'No, not that fork either'. This attempt to pass me 'that' fork continues to be a challenge, until you finally think to ask me 'to which fork are you referring?' Not until you can identify what I want will you be able to retrieve it with accuracy. This idea applies to any and everything. Could a guy succeed at finding what he has failed to identify? Sure he could, but he may not know what he has found.

To clarify, the struggle to attain Love could be due to the inability of the searcher to identify what it is. We searchers of Love have been conditioned and have held on to the socially accepted idea(s) of Love. We have become accustomed to hardship, disappointment, and heartbreak; we've become used to the inability to eat, think or sleep. In our minds, if our mate is not terrified at the idea of losing us; or if our mate does not yell, scream or even become physically violent with us; if he or she can deal with our relationship objectively, then it is assumed that he or she does not Love us; as if to say that only a display animalistic behavior qualifies Love.

I have heard that Love is uncontrollable. I have heard that Love is an involuntary impulse under whose influence we are all sure to fall. In many examples, Love has been synonymous with martyrdom and/or sacrifice. Sacrifice or the idea of losing something in order to gain something has become a commonly promoted or suggested practice. I would argue though that a thing not valued is a thing not a loss at all. If a child who is crossing a street is about to be struck by a car, it will not be my intent to allow myself to be hit by a car and possibly killed to save the child. On the contrary, my intent would be to save us both from being hit by a car. If by chance I am hit and seriously injured and the child is saved, such an event qualifies as circumstantial. A circumstantial event is incidental. Sacrifice is an offering, and so is done on purpose. Who, absent a suicide mission, would seek to be hit by a car on purpose?

The idea that Love is synonymous with sacrifice is insane. It is no wonder that most relationships exist and/or end in disaster. There are so many people who fear relationships, because they foresee a need to sacrifice some part of themselves. You must understand that to sacrifice is a choice; it is not involuntary. This means that the wounds that you acquired via your relationships are self-inflicted. Contemplate this for a moment.

In regards to an earlier statement that I made (a thing not valued is a thing not a loss at all), if what is to 'change' fails to compare in value to the thing gained, then there is no loss. Be ever mindful that change and loss, though appearing related, are not the same phenomenon. Change is characterized by a transformation or a mutation, whereby something improves or not. Loss on the other hand suggests the unexpected absence of a thing of value, never to be recovered or found (again).

It is usually a challenge to eliminate an illness if the unhealthy party is unaware of her condition. Take a moment to consider your condition. Consider the possibility that a misunderstanding of Love has prevented you from realizing it (Love). In the next chapter we will probe deeper in an attempt to determine just how off based we may be.

A suggestion: re-read this chapter once more to be sure that the idea communicated is fully understood. Once you have a decent grasp of what is being said, move on to the next chapter.

THE ADDICTION

A former associate of mines asked me a question a while ago. She said: 'I understand that you argue that Love is not involuntary; but what about the initial attraction you feel towards a person? Isn't that involuntary?'

This was an excellent question. My response to her was as follows: 'Yes, the very initial attracting moment may appear involuntary; but once you have become cognizant of the attraction, it is no longer involuntary, because your 'Will' has become a factor and your ability to make a choice about whether to act on the attraction or not is immediately present'.

In almost all cases, what is usually mistaken for Love is an acquired emotional dependency. Think back to a time when you first met a man or a woman whom you really, really liked. You see him, you respect his appearance plus his demeanor, and the desire to say hello and ask of his name steadily increases in intensity. Sometimes this intensity increases to a point where what was once an inconspicuous inspection of the person in question has now become an obvious inability to turn away; in fact, he sees you seeing him and he smiles. The fact that there is in you a desire to not be seen 'checking him out' validates the reality that the ability to choose is present. Consider this for a moment.

At any rate, after snapping out of the staring spell you finally work up the nerve to go over and say hello. He responds favorably, and thus begins a new opportunity for 'love' (notice the lower case 'L'). Days go by and you and your new beau (lol) are hitting it off great; so great even that time seems to escape you. We've all been here before. We all know the feeling. Think back to it; the excitement, the butterflies, *the suspension*'. This is the most amazing moment that most, if not all of us have ever experienced. The problem is, in just about every single case, this 'moment' is short lived.

After a couple of months of the butterflies, what was once a moment of excitement has now become one of terror. You have seen and spent time with him; spoke on the phone with him for what seems like an entire month (or two) straight. On the 61st day (or 62nd, depending on the months), you call him, but he does not answer. The day progresses and it's now been almost 24 hours since you've last talked to him, and still no returned phone call. All of a sudden your effort to connect is overshadowed by a concern about whether he's lost interest or not. When he does finally return your call over a day and a half or more later you question his absence. He provides an 'ok' explanation, but now feels obligated to report his activities to you whenever he's not in your presence. His temporary absence brings back to your mind your previous dissatisfying relationship(s). This memory invokes a fear of reliving past hurts, and so you 'tighten your noose'.

What must be understood is that from 'this point on' the effort has now become one to prevent the loss of your relationship. We, as result of our conditioning, move from a desire to connect to a fear of losing the connection that we believe we've established. Be sure to remain attentive here, because *here* is where most of us fall off the wagon.

I repeat: our desire to connect transforms into a desperate effort to avoid losing the connection that we believe we've established.

Let's relate this scenario to a relatively simple example: you are at work and your boss asks you to come outside and assist him with a rather large safe that he is trying to move into the building. Your boss has created a ramp by laying a sheet of plywood up and across the steps. The objective is to push the safe up the ramp and onto the platform, so that the safe could be wheeled into the building. Your boss has tied a rope around the safe, so that he might pull the safe from the front. He has asked you to simultaneously push the safe from behind. Your boss has expressed to you his doubts about whether he would be able to move the safe up the ramp absent your help. On the first effort the rope slips from your boss' hands a little and the safe rolls backwards towards you. This has frightened you a bit. On the second effort, your boss is pulling the safe, but notices that it isn't budging. He looks behind the safe and he realizes that for fear of injury, you are reluctant to provide the safe an adequate push. The result: the safe remains outside at the bottom of the steps. Your boss, who is dissatisfied with your effort, fires you and replaces you with a stronger, more dependable employee. Initially you were ok with being fired, because it beats getting injured; until you realize that you no longer had an income and could no longer afford your cost of living. If only you had made a sincere effort to push forward.

A very simple example, but I hope that the principle idea is understood. In the event that you did not understand, allow me to provide you an even simpler example: if you and I are holding opposite ends of a string of yarn, an effort to connect, which is characterize by both of us moving forward towards each other would pose no threat to the string; but if we each begin to pull in opposite directions, the string which initially held us together will eventually break. Your push to connect becomes a pull to secure your connection. So often a fear of loss **becomes our motive** for holding on.

Emotion is an impulse that surfaces as a result of some kind of stimulation; meaning it is a 'reaction' and in many cases a conditioned response. Emotion is not a direct or purposeful action. The emotional connection that one establishes with another does not happen until after a more subtle initial contact of sorts is made. Happiness is usually the result of some pleasant surprise or expected or unexpected excitement or fulfillment. Fear on the other hand surfaces due to concerns about loss (of persons, things valued, etc.).

The American Heritage Medical Dictionary defines emotion as '*an intense mental state that arises subjectively <u>rather than through conscious effort and is often accompanied by physiological changes.</u>*'

By this definition it can be determined that emotional reactions are fueled by internal or external stimuli. Many of us are so emotionally conditioned, that our emotional impulses <u>replaces</u> our intelligence; so much so that this 'fuzzy fluffiness' (i.e., emotion) becomes the defacto director(s) of our thoughts and behavior. My how easy it is for the practical mind to fall asleep. This reminds me of a statement I once read. The statement was made by Carlo Suares in his book The Cipher Genesis. I have added to and thereby simplified the statement for easy absorption. The statement goes:

'Life is to always be prevented from receiving perfect protection, shelter or comfort; for 'ease' causes complacency; thus trials and tribulations are needed to assure that the faculty of <u>adaptation</u> remains active; otherwise humanity will settle down lazily into a subhuman species.'

Our unwanting or sometimes wanting emotional dominance over our good sense perverts our thinking and vision. When the comfort or protection or security that we believe we've acquire via time spent with an ideal mate is disturbed, savage emotional and destructive (*sub-human*) behavior is usually the result. In the end, instead of growing closer to the person we <u>believe</u> we love; we pull and tug at them with hopes of avoiding loss; eventually 'popping the string' and destroying the connection or bind we once had.

The emotions of happiness and anger and all that lies in between might be caused by the principle of Love, but are most certainly not (Love). The trials and tribulations that we experience via our personal relationships can be quite frightening; but said experiences should never prevent us from living. Instead they should empower us all with the intelligence to make improve decisions in our future.

As with the previous chapter, re-read and understand before moving on to the next.

THE WEDGE

Below are a couple of definitions collected from the Merriam-Webster Online Dictionary. My reason for listing these definitions is to provide clarity of the below-mentioned concepts, so to empower the reader with the ability to discern whether or not the ideas discussed in this chapter are applicable to him or her.

Indecision is defined as *the inability to make a decision; a wavering between two or more possible courses of action.*

Apprehension is defined as *the fear that something bad or unpleasant is going to happen; a feeling of being worried about the future.*

Often times, despite the demonstrated excitement associated with the encountering of an opportunity for a new relationship, we enter said relationships in such a way that assures the relationships' failure from the very beginning. The experiences acquired via our past relationships were so emotionally traumatic and so debilitating that any opportunities for success in our future relationships are severely hindered.

The negative impact of our past circumstances causes us to enter our new situations with absolute apprehension. Our fear of reliving past hurts prevents us from committing to our new relationships completely. Though we know that our commitment is not 100%, we demand 100% commitment on the part our mates; and if we recognize that our mate's commitment is even slightly less than what we expect we verbally attack and sometimes even condemned our mate with the greatest of emotional-fire and hypocrisy. In our heart or hearts we aspire to be <u>all in</u>, but our efforts towards self-preservation and our preference to avoid reliving traumatic experiences of the past prevents us from totally committing.

The fear of loss, disappointment, etc., is some of the greatest deterrents to a successful relationship. The desire to preserve one's self becomes greater than the aspiration to fully connect with our mate; and even though the persons in question are well aware of the fact that their lack of commitment has contributed to the disruption of their relationship, they respond to the relationships failure as if they are totally oblivious about what caused said failure.

Entering into a new relationship with the predetermined idea regarding the eventual failure of the relationship assures the same.

A guy who has experienced disappointment in love enters a new relationship. He is very excited about his new situation, but his distrust for women causes him to second guess the relationship's potential. He doesn't realize it, but his apprehension and indecision is recognized by his new mate. This revelation has now caused her to become just as apprehensive and indecisive; and so from the very beginning a wedge established between the two. Unbeknownst to our lovely couple, their relationship is probably already over.

There are so many relationships that follow this exact same path, so understandably breakup or divorce rates are incredibly high. The inability of the individual to exercise discipline (emotionally), coupled with an unwillingness to take responsibility for the behavior or actions that are the result of this emotional instability all but guarantees repeat failures in personal relationships.

The average relationship is nothing more than an indefinite duration of manipulation, dishonesty, infidelity, dissatisfaction, distaste and indifference. Add to this a reluctance caused by a fear of the aforementioned, and the root of our relationships' evil (i.e. our disastrous thoughts and destructive behavior) becomes ever so clear.

What we have here is a chronic misunderstanding resulting from our ignorance of the principle of Love. We endeavor to find the solution or answer to this ever evasive riddle in others who are just as clueless on the subject as we are. I refer to this condition as 'chronic' because this ignorance is like a plague and it is obviously contagious. <u>A drastic change in our thinking</u> has to take place if we are to ever have a chance to truly experience Love.

Keep in mind that the first step towards recovery is to admit that there is a problem in the first place. Once the cause of the problem is determined, let us be disciplined and responsible enough to <u>correct</u> this problem.

As with the previous chapters, consider this for a moment before moving onto the next chapter.

JUST A BABY

A man and a woman who may or may not be complete strangers realize a mutual attraction between the two of them. They exchange pleasantries and eventually decide to go on a date. After about a month or more of dating the two agree to take their friendship to the next level. They both have made the determination that they each are ready for a monogamous relationship, and so they pledge their commitment to one another.

Both of the individuals in question have experienced relationships before, and so each individual naturally should know what's required for relationship to be successful; or at least that is what they think. One of the usual conversations in a relationship is the one where each individual tells the other person their likes and dislikes. The reason for sharing this information is to alert the other person to what he or she should and should not do. The relationship is new and so a mutual respect for each person's position is displayed. Past relationship experiences have obviously proven a failure; this is validated by the fact that the two have just entered a new relationship together. The understanding of what to do and what not to do, each person feels they have gained from their previous experiences. The unfortunate thing is that the fear of disappointment acquired from each person's past relationships causes each person to hold their ideals about what is required for a successful relationship as the absolute standard; if for no other reason than to secure themselves. Because the relationship is new, neither person wants to say anything to offend the other. As a result certain ideals about which this new couple unknowingly disagrees, remains.

A few months or more has passed and our new couple appears to be doing okay. There are at times though, bickering over certain ideals that the two never initially found a common ground on. The issues about which they disagree are essentially swept under the rug with the hopes that they will never surface again.

About a year into the relationship she becomes a bit agitated, because he is behaving in a way that is dissatisfying to her. Opposite that, he too is becoming more and more agitated because she is displaying behavior that is equally dissatisfying to him. Ultimately, each person is demanding a specific type of performance from the other. Here is where it gets interesting. Up until this point neither of these individuals have ever had a successful relationship; again, validated by the fact that just a year ago they entered into this then new relationship together. Each of these persons uses their past experiences (i.e. relationships) as <u>an absolute reference</u> for how to have successful relationship. Go figure, considering that all they have ever experienced in their past relationships was failure. At best the only thing that each of these individuals can offer a new relationship is ideas to assure that efforts to destroy their relationship are successful. Had either of them known the solution to a successful relationship while in their past situations, the two might have never even met.

What is often taken for granted and that is if it is even ever considered, is the fact that when two people meet they are absolute strangers. Even if two persons have 'known' each other for a respectable number of years, they have never known each other intimately. The tendency of the emotions to dominate intelligence causes persons to leap haphazardly into relationships; or once in the relationship, causes the person to treat their new relationship with soiled hands.

Consider this: each person on this planet is original. Most people are severely condition by their environment. Even our ideas about relationships and therefore love are the result of familial and societal conditioning. As a result, we each have an idea about how <u>we believe</u> a person should behave while in a relationship. To enter a relationship with a predetermined idea about how this complete stranger (your new partner) should behave is irresponsible and reckless. The responsibility required to actually understand the stranger is never contemplated. As a result, attempts to squeeze your new mate into a 'box' are futile. Simply put, the couple would have to reach an agreement regarding what they determine to be acceptable behavior in their relationship.

What you have in a potential new relationship is two very different individuals working to join together and ultimately creating <u>a third thing</u>, which is totally different from the previous two. In other words, on one hand you have an individual with experiences intact; and on the other hand you have a different individual with experiences intact. The <u>blending</u> of these two very different individuals is no different than the blending of two chemical agents; the result of which will either be successful or disastrous. When two people who are strangers intimately attempt to join together what must be understood is that the third thing (i.e. the relationship) that is created is in fact 'new' like an infant. Can you imagine what would happen if a new born baby who is just entering this world was expected to immediately stand, walk and fend for himself? What if you just started a new job and the person who hired you expected you to perform despite the fact that you are unskilled? In principle, it is with this same type of carelessness that the average person treats a new relationship. The inability to realize that the relationship is in fact new; that the blend of these two strangers ultimately <u>creates a third stranger</u> that neither of the initial two (strangers) really understand, is the reason why most couples never establish love.

In a new relationship it is one thing for each person to try to learn and understand the other; but it is a totally different thing to learn and understand what <u>the character of this blend</u> would be (like). As mentioned, a new relationship is like an infant. It has to be nurtured; it has to be learned and understood; it has to be trained or guided. The two people responsible for the creation of the relationship have to agree about its direction and have to do so with clean hands; meaning without the baggage from past relationships. While there are certainly valuable lessons that we each can and should carry from our past relationships, we cannot make the assumption that each new relationship will wear the lessons the same way. More importantly, the lessons that I acquire from my past circumstances should serve as a guide for me to follow. I should not seek to force my lessons on my new mate; for she has her own lessons to follow. Ideally, the two of us will create new lessons that neither of us has experienced yet. It might be productive for us to share our lessons if we choose, in an effort to find that common place between them. This is one way that we can begin to shape an agreed upon direction for our new situation. I like to use simple examples in my explanations to make it easier for the reader to comprehend complex ideas. One such example is the nurturing of or caring for an infant/child. Think about the time and consideration required to care for a life. Think of how she must be clothed, fed, guided and protected. Nothing relative to this newborn baby's ability or potential should be taken for granted. Such negligence would assure injury or worse. What I am suggesting is that the same <u>deliberate intent</u>, attention, responsibility and disciplined with which one would care for a baby is what is required to assure a healthy and durable relationship. The key word is deliberate.

The idea(s) discussed in this chapter requires serious consideration, because it demands a change in how you think about your relationship(s). A relationship viewed differently, is a relationship that will be treated or cared for differently. Take your time and sincerely try to learn your significant other. Find the areas where you differ and try to identify a silver lining. Some may consider what I am suggesting too technical and/or too demanding; nobody really wants to be disciplined. We all want utopia absent responsibility. Stop treating your new relationship as if it is an adult, ready to tackle the world. It is not an experienced adult; it is an infant. It will not jump up and work automatically; it requires your attention and constant guidance in order to mature. Anything short of this will only afford you more of the same.

As with the previous chapters, re-read and understand before moving forward.

FEELING LONELY

It is natural for a human being to desire companionship. From the time a person reaches puberty the quest for someone other than their family to love them dominates their thinking, and to that end, heavily influences their behavior.

Behind the smoking mirrors what we each seek is balance leading to equilibrium, which cannot be achieved by an individual alone.

Within nature its elements continually seek to combine, masculine with feminine, and by this process all that is life is perpetuated. To the contrary, absent this marriage of the elements, life would be naught.

With this understood, it is clear why so many men and women, who are the personifications of these masculine and feminine elements, seek happiness via relationships. In fact, it is often the opinion of some that true happiness is not possible absent a fulfilling relationship.

To 'relate' by definition implies *the seeking to identify* *shared characteristics* *by which a determination can be made regarding to which group a thing belongs* (Merriam-Webster).

The intent therefore of the individual who is seeking to relate to someone is to identify similar or shared characteristics so to effectively and 'more accurately' connect with them. This aspiration to connect registers in the mind of the individual as a mere impulse, but is in fact the natural order of things. The word order suggests structure or 'plan'. That being the case, it may be worth it to revisit an earlier conversation from chapter two of this book, where I answer the question of an acquaintance. The dialog went as follows:

'A former associate of mines asked me a question a while ago; she said, 'I understand that you argue that Love is not involuntary; but what about the initial attraction you feel towards a person? Isn't that involuntary?'

This was an excellent question. My response to her was as follows: "Yes, the very initial attracting moment may appear involuntary; but once you have become cognizant of the attraction, it is no longer involuntary, because your 'Will' has become a factor and your ability to make a choice about whether to act on the attraction or not is immediately present'.

Although the initial movement is considered to be an impulse, and although nature continuously guides a Man or Woman to attract with the intent to connect, you must understand that the Will of Man (or Woman) determines what action occurs.

Understanding that in each of us lies the aspiration to connect with another, it is conceivable that a person might feel lonely and unfulfilled when not in a relationship. So many people have experienced repeat disappointment and have become so fearful of being hurt, that they find themselves without companionship more often than not. It is quite a dynamic circumstance when you think about it. Your strong desire to connect with a person is disturbed by your equally strong desire to preserve yourself (emotionally). What a conundrum.

Often times the desire to connect falls into desperation; the outcome is usually the lowering of what we have established as our standards. In the end we choose to indulge in a situation where we fail to find complimentary characteristics. The dissatisfaction of these types of situations are determined early on in the relationship, but our fear of being without a mate causes us 'look past' what we qualify as flaws in the other person. Months, maybe even years go by when the distaste and indifference outweighs our fears and we finally admit what we have known for so long to be true, 'that there is no longer a connection; that there is no more love'.

Further consideration though would help us to realize that what actually cemented us or glued us together was our emotion, which isn't a bad thing; but it serves as a weak connection if the things that we have deemed most important were not a part of the equation. The things that I speak of are those things or ideas about which we knew early on there was no connection (for). When we finally call it quits we feel that we have wasted time again on yet another unfulfilling relationship. Eighty-five percent of the population lacks any real understanding of themselves. That being said, what is often presented by one person when meeting another is a personality that has been rehearsed and/or crafted over many years; over many experiences. One's character is those traits about them which are consistent, even absent an audience. The character is that inner part of you that knows the true reasons for all that you do. Personality on the other hand is one's crafted ideas of himself that he presents to the world. Personality is usually characterized by an inflated (or deflated) sense of self-importance. The personality becomes our protection, our shield behind which we hide those things about ourselves that we have determined to be inadequate. With eighty-five percent of the population living their life out through their personality, that could mean that 8 ½ out if 10 people who might approach you in a given moment for whatever reason are insincere in their approach; meaning they are not being forthcoming about their 'real' reason for approaching you, or their presentation and/or dialog is disingenuous. This is especially true in personal relationships.

When initially meeting, each person who is a part of this would-be couple puts on their best face and best performance in hopes of impressing and attracting the object of their affection. It may be based on this performance that either person decides to give the other the benefit of the doubt. After a while she grows so used to his physical attractiveness, that she no longer admires it. He has 'captured' the object of his affection, and so the hard work is over. He lets his guard down and the theatrical performance fades. His beauty has become a mere fixture in their home to the point where it is no longer noticed. The interesting thing about these shallow relationships is that once the infatuation period passes the only thing left is the dialog that is coming out of his mouth. She now notices things about him and/or his conversation that she didn't notice before (or chose to ignore before); things that in most instances would be a deal breaker for her. These characteristics of his that move in contradistinction to hers are a turn off, and so the jig is up and the relationship is over.

Care has to be taken when considering a relationship. We have to be sure that our desire to connect with someone, anyone, doesn't fall into desperation. We dislike so much these feelings of loneliness that we would do anything or accept almost anyone to take our minds off of the fact that we have not found satisfaction in our relationships. The dissatisfaction within which we live is OUR creation and is the result of OUR own negligence. Imagine the demand you often make for someone to not be careless with your heart, when you are.

Re-read, consider and move on.

BEING ALONE

This next subject matter I cannot necessarily qualify as factual. At best it must be considered a philosophy. The subject matter to which I am referring is the idea of feeling lonely versus being alone. Since the topic of feeling lonely was considered in the last chapter there is no need to rehash it here.

Often times when a person has ended a relationship he or she begins to feel the need for companionship in a relatively short amount of time. Based on my experience and in my opinion, being alone can be truly rewarding in a number of respects.

A Time to Think

One obvious benefits of being alone is the amount of time that a person has to think and/or reflect on all past choices and circumstances. While it is certainly a challenge for many of us to be alone, it is very necessary if it is the intent of a person to put experiences and their current relationship standing into perspective. In a previous publication that I wrote titled the Key to Character, I referenced a situation where, after a breakup, a person misses her ex-partner. When thoroughly considered, she realizes that the emotional discomfort that she is experiencing is more related to her own fears of being alone or her fears of seeing her ex-partner with a new partner. Ultimately, any effort to rekindle this situation is selfish in principle, because the goal is for the person in question to eliminate her own pain and discomfort.

Having the time to evaluate past choices in an effort to determine where we may have gone wrong is absolutely therapeutic. To realize that our initial errors took place at the very beginning of the relationship helps us to understand that such a disingenuous beginning laid the foundation for our past relationship's failure. Instead of thinking woe is me our thoughts become shame on me.

A chance to re-organize

Another benefit of being alone, once one has reflected on past choices, is the opportunity to reorganize one's thoughts and priorities. In any instance where a past behavior is discarded and replaced by a more progressive behavior a chance for a new beginning is upon you. Bad relationships as we all know are very distracting. While experiencing a bad relationship we often times neglect everything, from our friends to our jobs, to our bills, and even our children. Being alone and having the time to reorganize allows us a chance to eliminate the toxic residue, of not only the previous past relationship, but of all past toxic relationships. We've all been there before whether in larger or small measure, we're we feel as if 1000 pounds of pressure has been lifted from our shoulders. Just imagine that 1000 pounds of pressure being lifted and never ever returning again. Trust me, it is real freedom.

Be discriminative

Now that you have reflected and you have cleansed yourself or refined your thinking; and now that you have reorganized your ideas about yourself, your chosen direction and about what you want out of a relationship, you are ready for a new opportunity. This is where responsibility is very important, as it is up to you to be discriminative in determining who might be worthy of what you have to contribute to a relationship. You must be brave enough to discuss all matters of importance for you from the onset; even if that means that the object of your affection walks away. You must be willing to stand firm while simultaneously displaying willingness to compromise. You must effectively contribute to the suggested direction of your new relationship. You must be aware; you must be in the moment; you must be present. You must not bring yesterday's fears into today's progress.

Make intelligent choices

Lastly, cleaning and reorganizing your thinking, and exercising discrimination empowers you with the ability to make intelligent decisions. If you are not a smoker and if you do not like smoke you do not ignore the fact that the person you are interested in is a smoker. You must be disciplined and be responsible enough to walk away. If you are a woman who does not respect abusive name-calling, domestic violence, etc., and you recognize any of these traits in a potential mate must be disciplined and responsible enough to walk away. The message here is very simple. The value of alone time cannot be overstated; especially when considering matters of the heart. Be strong, be intelligent, and 'treat your heart' the way that you would expect others to treat it.

As with the other chapters, reread, and understand before moving on.

LOVE

What is love? Love is not a thing that can be captured. Love is not an emotion; neither happiness nor sadness. Love is not an inability to control one's thinking. Love is not an inability to eat, sleep, work, or play. Love is not a gross display of animalist (emotional) outburst. So, what is Love?

Love is a process whereby two separate and/or different entities seek union with a goal of becoming one (entity). Love is attraction; for the principle of attraction is the process whereby two are drawn together to form one. Love is perfection or the best part. Love is the key between opposites; for it is the 'middle' that solves the riddle of extremes. Love is expressed or demonstrated in a number of ways: a common ground, a handshake, communication, compromise, even a child is the expression of Love. Each of the aforementioned are the sum total of two or more extremes. A compromise provides a legitimate "win-win" situation. In a sincere compromise there is no loss suffered on either side. The compromise provides the best case scenario or the perfect outcome. Love is that compromise. Love is the best possible outcome, because with actual Love there is no loss suffered on either side. The joining of the two to perfectly become one provides the best case scenario for both people when proper care has been taken. God, who is arguably the sum total of all things, seen or unseen, is Love (literally). Love is not an involuntary impulse, but is in fact a purposeful or deliberate action. The keywords here are "deliberate" and "action"; for love is an action verb (not a noun). This means that your effort to achieve union with another is done on purpose. To do a thing on purpose requires that you are aware, or attentive and in the moment. This awareness makes you absolutely responsible for the outcome of your relationship.

Think about this for a moment.

From here on out there is no need for the reader of these words to suffer a moment more. You the reader should now know and understand what is required to actually establish Love. Love does not happen and sustain itself automatically, despite what many may think. Love requires work. There is no magic involved outside of the deliberate exercising of your Will. I am sure that many of you will feel that the ideas expressed here 'takes all of the fun' out of Love. I'd respond to this statement by asking, considering the repeat disappointment you've experienced, how much fun have you really had?

Love is a choice, not a prison sentence. To understand that your dissatisfaction in your current relationship is the result of a choice you've made means that you should understand that you could just as easily choose better.

From the moment I thought about writing this book I said that it would have one of two effects: either it would empower an individual to more effectively invest in his or her relationship thereby making it better, or it will empower a person with the Will to walk away. The ideas expressed herein will be quite frightening to many, especially to those who have found comfort in mediocrity. In the minds of some this small book will qualify as no more than a disturbance of what they have deemed an ideal situation. For others it shall serve as a liberator; freeing them from the isles of confusion, uncertainty, disappointment and despair. Empowering them with the ability to shape and manage each and every aspect of their relationships and their life.

In the human family there are hundreds of things that we each have in common; but one of the more valuable of our abilities is often taken for granted; that being our inalienable right to choose.

In every waking moment each and every human being on this planet exercises the power of choice 'millions of times per day'. We have though, developed a habit of suspending that power of choice when it is most needed.

Love or the union of opposites is the natural order of things; it is nature's law. Let us be ever mindful of the power of Love and let us be responsible and diligent, aware and disciplined in our choice making; forever keep in mind that Love is now and will forever be the Law; but Love should always be established under Will.

"Love is the Law; Love under Will."

IN SUMMARY

The Longest chord is another name for the diameter of a circle. In mathematics, a chord is a line that connects any two points on an arch of a circle. The diameter, which is established via the center of a circle, is considered to be the longest chord of a circle, because the distance between two points on an arch of a circle is greatest at its center.

Relative to our discussion in this book, the idea of a circle corresponds to an individual's circumstances. Each of our individual worlds; each of our individual ideas or thoughts; each of our families, friends, work environments, our homes, are our respective circles.

To find the diameters of these circles is to discover the causes, the strengths or weaknesses and ultimately the solutions to these circles.

Despite the fact that all of our various challenges appear to be different on the surface, what lies at the center of each and every troubling issue, regardless of appearances, is essentially the same.

The Key to Character is about identifying with one's core: the "true you" as opposed to your daily presentations or extra performances. NOW is an effort to help you to see that the solution to extremes or that the answer to your problems, or the key to the two points furthest apart on a given circle, lies at the center of said circle. Love Under Will communicates to you that "Love is that centermost point" in a circle. It is the cause and therefore the solution or the answer to the riddle of extremes.

Each of these three books appear to discuss different issues, but when thoroughly considered, one should come to the conclusion that there is a connection or one central theme or principle idea that stretches from the very beginning of this book to its end. A theme that is always consistent, no matter the appearance. A theme that proves that between any two points, any two circles, or multiple circles even, a diameter can be found. This diameter is the proverbial "correct path" upon which each and every one of us MUST travel. This path, this journey is an extremely long one. This is the path towards our salvation; it's the Longest Chord.

About the Author

Khalid Bey has been an active community member where he is located for over 20 years and an employee within government for several years now. With an educational background in the Social Sciences, Khalid continues to use his talents an author and a public speaker. He has lectured about man's personal identity, human behavior, human relationships and government. Now an author of eight published books (three of which are contained in this book), Khalid Bey clearly has a lot to offer. Stating his recent realization of his passion for empowering others, Khalid Bey says 'who would imagine that empowering others and seeing others do well could be so satisfying'. His works continues to win favor with readers. When ask what it is that he aspires to do more than all else, he replied *to understand and inspire*.   Khalid's passion to empower people, neighborhoods, and communities, continue to be the driving force behind his efforts. An insightful Man, Khalid lives by his coined slogan, "In order to change the world, all one has to do is change his mind". Be on the lookout for much more from this inspiring author.

Deyel Publishing
Syracuse, New York
United States of America